WHITE TRUFFLE
YORKSHIRE PUDDING

I would like to thank very much Jeannie Swales for her time and excellent ability in helping me put my recipes into words.

Tony Bartholomew for photographing (and eating!) the dishes I chose to do. The photos are amazing as you will see.

A big thank-you to Sir Alan Ayckbourn for kindly writing a brilliant foreword.

Thanks to Mr Martin Simpson for supplying the photo of the shoot, and the game he let me eat afterwards.

Special thanks to Rachel, without whom I wouldn't be here!

Copyright Giorgio Alessio, 2005
Photographs copyright Tony Bartholomew, 2005
Editor Jeannie Swales

Published by La Trifula Publishing

The moral right of the author has been asserted

ISBN 0-9549753-0-8

Design by Anonymous Design
Printed in Great Britain by Spellman Walker

Foreword

One night in 1973, we were walking home from the Library Theatre after an evening show - most probably, now I come to think of it, a performance of one of *The Norman Conquests*. On that occasion, our route home from Vernon Road took us along Queen Street.

To our amazement, we passed a truly rare sight, a new restaurant apparently open after eight o'clock at night. For, truth be told, at that time there were precious few to be found - the Royal Hotel's Gourmet Restaurant being one notable exception.

Which was odd, considering it was a town which during the summer months regularly played host to half a dozen or so theatre companies, many of whom hungrily prowled the nocturnal Scarborough streets in vain search of a post-show evening meal. The rule at that period was very much fish and chips or nothing. Which, even for the greatest fish and chip aficionado among the luckless theatricals, after three months and five costume alterations...

Anyway, on this particular night, we peered through this magical restaurant's windows like Victorian orphans ogling a sweet shop. Could the place indeed be open? At 10.30? *pm?* There indeed in the back was a group, apparently the staff, eating, drinking and chatting away. In response to our enquiring looks they cheerfully waved us in.

As we ate the first of countless memorable Italian meals, I remember remarking that, having made this discovery, it was our sworn duty to keep this place open, whatever the cost, even if it meant single-handedly eating here every night. What dedication! Such sacrifice!

And I seem to remember we did, at least for the first month or so, often - until word spread - the only people there.

Now, 32 years, one change of ownership and heaven knows how many meals and bottles of good wine later we continue to treasure the Lanterna and secretly still think of it as our restaurant.

My recipe for the good life is to have a job you love, a home you're happy in, a town you like living in and a first rate restaurant just round the corner. How lucky we are.

Sir Alan Ayckbourn CBE

Introduction

My interest in, and love of, anything to do with food and cooking came naturally from home. My mum is a very, very good cook, and watching, and learning from her, probably started me on the career path I chose. On my dad's side, relatives had a restaurant in my home town of Moncalvo: some said it was one of the best restaurants in Piemonte. We were always visiting, and even when I was little, I would help out. It gave me an early insight into how restaurants worked.

When I came over here, it seemed that Italian restaurants would have dishes from practically every region of Italy on their menus - and it's a vast country. I find it hard to cover the dishes of just my region, let alone all the other areas. And, to many British people, Italian food means pizza - but a pizza in Italy is a snack, not a meal. Then again, it's certainly not junk food, not if it's done properly with freshly-baked bread, fresh tomatoes and cheese!

I think it's important that children should know more about the food they eat: where it comes from, and the importance of good food. When children are given salty, convenience foods, like crisps, at an early age, they can quickly lose their palate.

In Italy the only time you see anybody eating crisps is with *aperitivi*, certainly not as part of a child's packed lunch box! Parents should lead by example - when my son was young, he loved eating fruit after his meal because I did, and I did because I was brought up to do it.

It's also important that we learn to resist the pressure of TV commercials, and supermarkets. We are buying more and more prepacked foods from supermarkets, rather than using the delicious, seasonal foods which are literally on our doorsteps. I have always been influenced by my experience of shopping in Italy for food. I love going to the markets for fresh fruit and veg (every Thursday is market day in the square in Moncalvo).

These days, even in a seaside town like Scarborough, we have only two or three fishmongers left: people seem to prefer to buy exotic fish from supermarkets and smoked fish that looks like it has been painted with yellow paint - leaving the smoking houses to close down. (I have used sea fish for many of the recipes in this book, as the Lanterna is near the sea, but I have also tried to encourage the use of fresh water fish: the stocks in the sea need time to regenerate.)

People are afraid of old-fashioned, nutritious food because it looks different. Tongue and ox-tail don't look like prime cuts such as fillet steak, and people sometimes ask me if they're edible!

The reason I wrote this book was to show the Italian and Piemontese way of cooking, with Scarborough in the middle, because I live here and can buy wonderful prime local products, which are sometimes taken for granted. There are odd ingredients which aren't local, like truffles, but you can still buy them from specialist shops.

The aim is to use good, fresh local ingredients, and to persuade people that good food need not be complicated. If you don't believe me, just take a look at the egg and truffle recipe on page 19 - nothing could be easier, or more delicious!

Enjoy the book.

Giorgio Alessio

Contents

basics   page 11

starters   page 15

mains   page 25

puddings   page 71

index   page 79

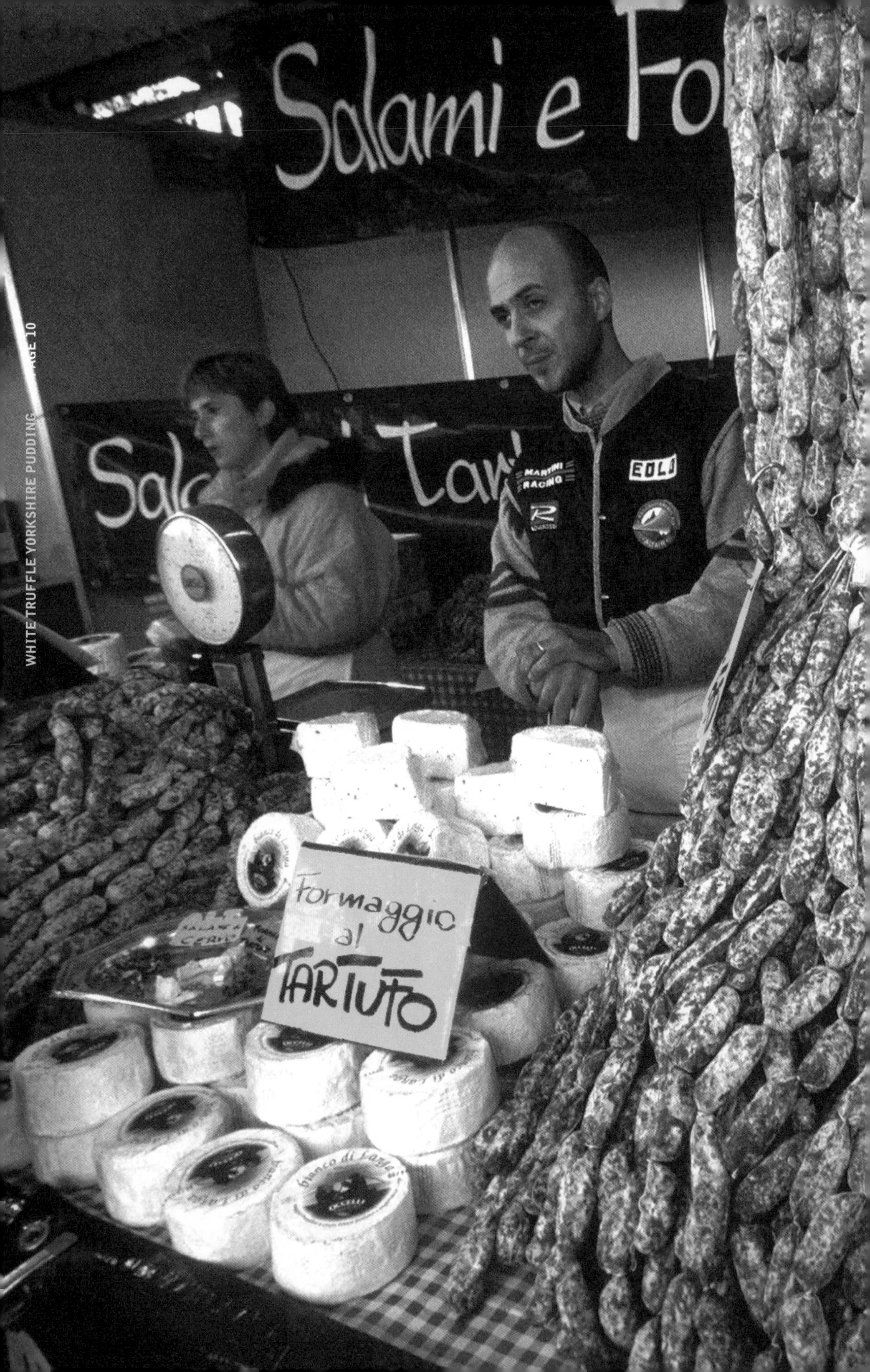
Salami e
Formaggio al TARTUFO
MARTINI RACING
EOLO

stock

All the recipes make approximately
two litres of stock

Chicken

2 raw chicken carcasses
2 sticks of celery
1 small whole onion
2 medium carrots, scraped
2 bay leaves, fresh or dried
2 pinches salt
1 pinch white pepper

Place all the ingredients in a stockpot or large pan
with four litres of water, and allow to simmer
gently for two to three hours. Do not allow to
boil, as this will darken the stock. Allow to cool,
then strain before use.

Beef

As chicken, but using two beef shin bones, each
cut into four pieces and, if possible, with the
marrowbone still in.

Simple vegetable stock

2 carrots, scraped and finely chopped
2 sticks of celery, finely chopped
1 small onion, finely chopped
5-6 fresh basil leaves
2 bay leaves, fresh or dried
5-6 fresh sage leaves
100g butter
2 pinches salt
1 pinch white pepper

In a stockpot or large saucepan, gently fry the
onions in the butter until transparent. Add the
celery and carrot and stir for a few seconds. Add
the water and remaining ingredients, and simmer
for two to three hours - again, don't allow to boil.
Cool and strain before use.

Fish stock

1 medium skate wing
6 scampi heads
2 cloves garlic
100g parsley, without stalks
Salt and pepper
1 onion
2 litres water

Put all the ingredients into a large pan and
simmer for ninety minutes (fish stock doesn't
need to simmer for as long as the other stocks).
Sieve the stock and allow to cool.

salsa alla besciamella
Bechamel, or white, sauce
Makes approximately 750ml

600ml milk
100g butter
50g '00' flour
Salt and pepper

Bring the milk to a simmer - do not allow to boil.
In another pan, melt the butter, then add the
flour slowly, stirring continuously. When
completely mixed, add the hot milk a little at a
time, again stirring continuously until all the milk
has been added, and you have a smooth sauce.
Season to taste with the salt and pepper.

pasta
Egg pasta
Makes approximately 800g, serves 6-8

The final consistency of this pasta will depend on
how much effort you're prepared to put in - the
firmer, the better. In Italy, the man of the family
often used to finish the mixing: the firmer it gets,
the harder the dough is to work!

500g '00' flour
5 medium free range eggs, beaten

In a large mixing bowl add the flour, make a well
in the centre and add the eggs. Mix together by
hand until you have a firm dough. Allow to rest
for twenty minutes before using. For a richer
colour, replace the five eggs with four medium
eggs and three egg yolks. Roll out and cut to the
required shape.

yorkshire puddings
Makes 10

My friend who helped me write this book is a
true Yorkshirewoman, and reckoned she had
never tasted a Yorkshire pudding better than her
mother's - until she tried these! The secret is in
the teaspoon of cold water and the fine '00' flour,
which give the puddings a beautifully light
texture. These puddings really rise, so use a deep
muffin tin, rather than the traditional Yorkshire
pudding tin.

200g '00' flour
Pinch salt
3 medium eggs
400ml milk
1 teaspoon cold water
2 tablespoons vegetable oil

Beat together the flour, salt, eggs, milk and water
until smooth.

Pour a little vegetable oil into the bottom of each
muffin cup, just enough to cover the bottom. Put
the tray into a hot oven, about gas mark 9, 240
degrees C. When the oil starts to make a light
haze, remove from the oven. Carefully add the
batter, filling each cup to the rim. Put in the oven
for twenty to thirty minutes, or until golden.

WHITE TRUFFLE YORKSHIRE PUDDING

Starter

asparagi
Asparagus

We northern Italians love asparagus. There's a huge plantation at Poirino in Piemonte, and you may be surprised to hear that there are restaurants that open just for the asparagus season.

In this country, the asparagus season is very short - I would recommend only eating it from March to May, when its rich flavour is at its best. If you buy it out of season, it will almost certainly be imported, will have been picked before it's fully ripe and will have travelled a long way, all of which affect the flavour.

In some parts of France and Italy, they will use asparagus which isn't quite at its best, peeling it to make it more tender. But I prefer to use very good asparagus and leave the skin on. If the bottom of the stem is white, or woody, cut it off and just use the tips. Be sparing with sauces, otherwise you'll just drown the beautiful flavour of the vegetable.

The first of these three dishes was considered a Sunday treat when I was growing up in Piemonte. It's as simple as can be, but the flavours are stupendous.

For the second dish, try and get a very, very fresh young gorgonzola, which will be smooth and creamy. Don't go for something like dolcelatte - this cheese doesn't actually exist in Italy, it's just a trademark, a product which someone invented and passed off as an Italian cheese. I believe in real food, not something with an invented name!

The last of the three, tagliatelle agli asparagi, particularly represents for me what this book is all about: real, down-to-earth food, which is good for us, delicious and simple to cook. It's what cooking and eating should be all about!

For each of the following three recipes, simply stand the as aparagus in a tall pan of boiling water, with the tips clear of the water so they steam, and cook for five to six minutes, then drain.

asparagi tradizionali
A traditional Italian way with asparagus

SERVES 4

48 spears cooked asparagus
100g butter
4 eggs
100g parmesan cheese

Fry an egg per person in the butter, place on top of the plated asaparagus, and scatter with grated parmesan.

WHITE TRUFFLE YORKSHIRE PUDDING

Starter

asparagi con gorgonzola
Asparagus with gorgonzola

SERVES 4

48 spears cooked asparagus
100g gorgonzola cheese
50g white sauce (see page 12)
1 tablespoon vegetable stock (see page 11)

Melt the gorgonzola with a little white sauce and a tablespoon of stock to make a thin sauce, and use it to dress the asparagus. Alternatively, just put chunks of gorgonzola on top of the cooked asparagus, and melt under the grill.

tagliatelle agli asparagi
Tagliatelle with asparagus

SERVES 4

600g fresh pasta (see page 12)
24 spears asparagus
50g butter
1 clove garlic, finely chopped
50g parmesan cheese, grated
Salt and pepper

Steam the asparagus, then drain and cut into short lengths. Place in a pan with the butter and garlic and allow to sauté for a few minutes, then add the parmesan and a pinch of salt and pepper. Boil the fresh pasta until cooked, drain, and stir into the sautéed asparagus.

carpaccio di filetto
Marinated beef fillet

SERVES 6

People often think that carpaccio is a type of meat, but actually it refers to the cooking technique of marinating, or curing, in olive oil and lemon juice. You can use this technique on any flesh, including fish: swordfish and salmon both lend themselves well to carpaccio, and elsewhere in this book you can find an excellent recipe for carpaccio of sea trout.

This is another delicious way with raw meat and Yorkshire puddings. The heat of the Yorkshire puddings gently warms the fillet, and gives a beautiful flavour. Half Piemontese, half Yorkshire: the perfect combination!

500g beef fillet
50ml extra virgin olive oil
Juice of half a lemon
50g parmesan cheese
White truffle
Salt and pepper
6 Yorkshire puddings (see page 13)

Finely slice the beef, squeeze over the lemon juice and oil. Season with the salt and pepper. Leave to marinate for approx thirty minutes. Cover with shavings of parmesan cheese.

Starter

uovo al tegamino con tartufi bianchi
Eggs with white truffles

This is truly delicious, and yet is one of the easiest and most straightforward recipes imaginable. If you ordered this in a restaurant in Italy, you'd pay a fortune for it. I'm constantly tempted to put it on the menu at the Lanterna, but don't, because I'm afraid people would think it just too simple. But do try it at home - I promise you won't regret it! It's an absolutely classic truffle recipe - you don't make the grade as an Italian if you can't do this properly!

Per person:
1 or 2 eggs, depending on appetite
Butter
White truffle
Salt

Simply fry the eggs lightly in the butter, with a touch of salt on the whites, then generously shave over the white truffle.

pera cotta al vino rosso con salsa al gorgonzola e mascarpone
Baked pears in red wine with a sauce of two classic Italian cheeses

SERVES 6

Pears and cheese are as traditional a combination in Italy as apples and cheese are in Britain. There's an old Italian saying: *non far sapere al contadino come buono il formaggio con le pere*, or "don't tell the farmer how good the cheese is with the pears...", meaning that he would eat them all, and we'd never get to have any! I like to celebrate this combination with two classic cheeses, gorgonzola and mascarpone, and to cook the pears in a good, earthy, Barbera red wine.

200g white sauce (see page 12)
200g gorgonzola cheese, cut into small pieces
200g mascarpone cheese
3 large Williams pears
125ml glass red wine
1/2 glass Marsala wine
2 tablespoons brown sugar
Paprika

Put the white sauce in a saucepan, warm gently, then add the mascarpone and gorgonzola. Stir together to make a smooth sauce. Keep warm. Meanwhile, peel the pears, cut in half lengthways, and core. Place in a baking tray then pour over the red wine and Marsala and sprinkle with brown sugar.
Cover and place at the top of a hot oven, gas mark 7, 220 degrees C, for approximately fifteen to twenty minutes, until the pears have softened and have a brown/red colour.
Leaving the stalk end intact, place on a serving plate, slice the pear, and fan them. Pour the hot cheese sauce over and lightly sprinkle with paprika. Serve hot.

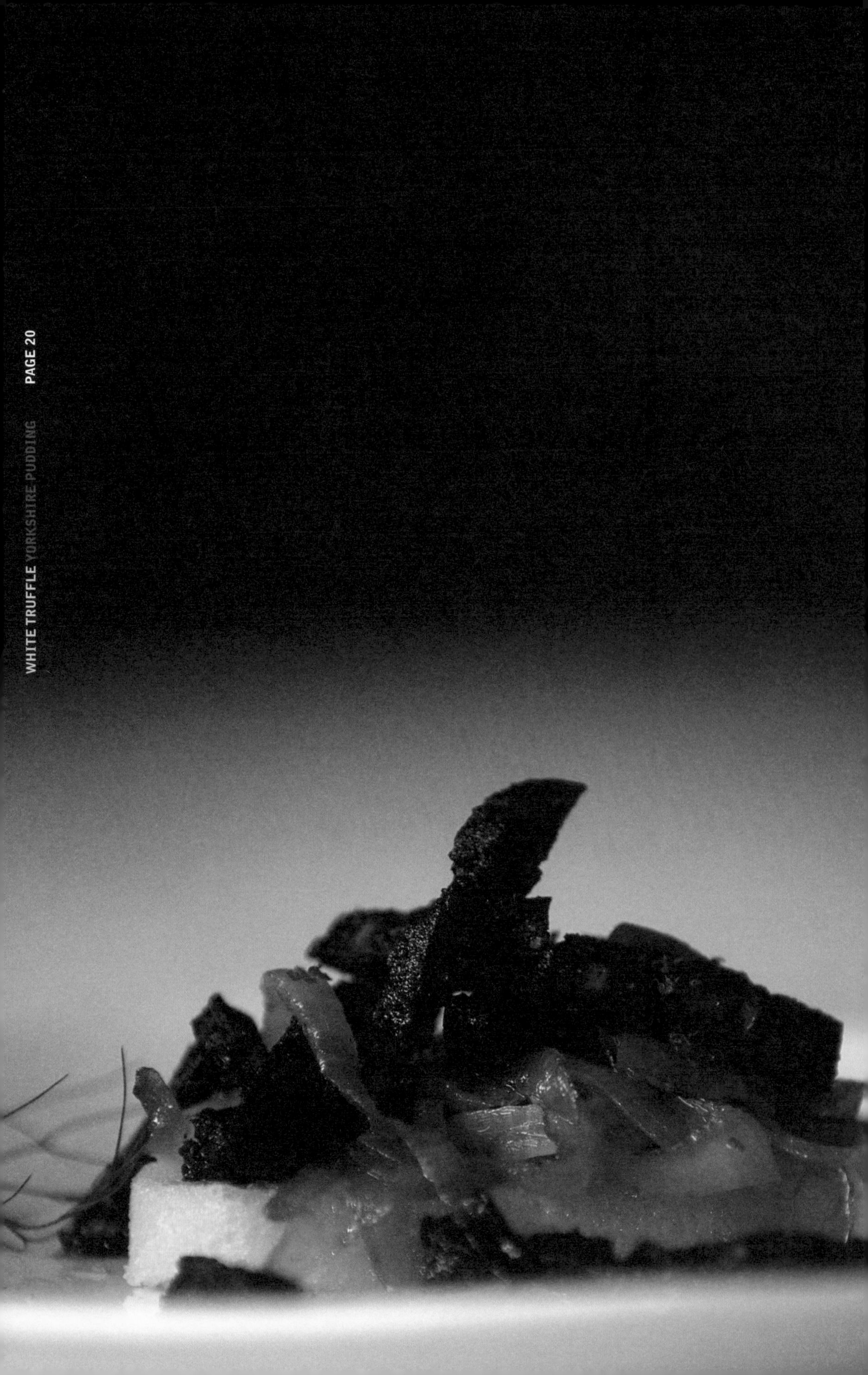

Starter

sanguinaccio con cipolle

Black pudding with onions

SERVES 4

This is a very typical northern Italian recipe, using lovely old-fashioned ingredients. We used to make this at home with boiled and set pigs' blood and onions, but you can recreate the dish with black pudding and polenta. It reminds me of home and my youth!

    1 onion, thinly sliced
    50g butter
    500g black pudding
    250g polenta
    Salt and pepper

Caramelize the onion in the butter until golden. Add the black pudding, sliced and then cut into strips, and cook for three to four minutes until tender.

Meanwhile, make the polenta. Bring one litre of water to the boil, add the polenta gradually, stirring continuously, and seasoning with the salt and pepper until it thickens to the consistency of mashed potato.

Serve immediately, spooning the polenta on to a plate and topping with the black pudding and onions. Alternatively, you can pour the polenta into a tray and allow it to cool, then slice it into portions. Put each portion on a plate and top with the black pudding and onions.

carpaccio di trota di mare affumicata

Carpaccio of smoked sea trout

SERVES 4

We all know now that it's good and healthy to eat as seasonally as possible. This is very seasonal, because the sea trout is only fished around Scarborough in the summer. Unfortunately, as with so many traditional skills, it's hard to find a smoking house these days. To the best of my knowledge, there are only a couple left around here, between Scarborough and Whitby. I believe - and I know I'm not alone - that we should be treasuri∞ng and preserving these old skills. So much better to buy properly smoked fish than that stuff you can buy in the supermarkets which looks as if it's been painted with yellow colouring and probably has!

This is a celebration of a British skill, smoking, and an Italian cooking method - carpaccio.

    400g finely sliced smoked sea trout
    Juice of 1 lemon
    50ml extra virgin olive oil
    Salt and freshly ground pepper

Place the trout on a serving plate. Drizzle over the lemon juice and then the oil, making sure the fish is evenly covered. Sprinkle with a pinch of salt and then a generous grinding of black pepper. Allow to marinate for at least thirty minutes before serving.

Starter

insalata di carne cruda alla monferrina

Raw meat salad Monferrato-style

SERVES 4

The British are traditionally a little reserved about raw meat, but, trust me, this is gorgeous! I like to serve this as a starter stuffed inside half a Yorkshire pudding per person (see page 13), or with crusty bread. Either way, add a glass of wine or two for a perfect antipasto!

> 300g lean veal
> 1 clove garlic, finely chopped
> Juice of 1 lemon
> Salt and pepper
> 50ml extra virgin olive oil

Mince the veal: the best, and most traditional way of doing this is to chop it as finely as possible with a knife, a technique known as *batutta a coltello*. Add the garlic, lemon juice, salt and pepper and oil. Mix togther, then refrigerate in a covered dish for at least four hours before serving.

trota in carpione

Pickled trout

SERVES 5-6

Traditionally, this recipe would be made using tench, a freshwater fish, but it's hard to come by in this country, so I've used trout instead. However, if you are lucky enough to find some tench, grab it and make this - it's delicious eaten cold, on a warm summer's evening - with, of course, a glass of nicely chillled white wine!

> 5 trout, 300-500g each
> Plain flour to coat
> Olive oil for frying
> 1 onion, chopped
> 1 carrot, chopped
> Pinch of parsley, chopped
> 2 cloves of garlic, minced
> 125ml dry white wine
> 125ml red wine vinegar
> Salt and pepper

Coat the trout with the flour, and fry in very hot oil for a couple of minutes each side. Place in a serving dish with the juices from the pan.

Put more oil into the same pan, add the onion, carrot, parsley and the garlic and fry gently for a few minutes. Then add the salt, pepper, wine and vinegar, and bring to the boil. Pour the resulting hot marinade over the fish.

Cover and allow to cool. Keep in the fridge for at least two days before eating, and eat very cold.

WHITE TRUFFLE YORKSHIRE PUB

Main

pasta con lumachine di mare

Egg pasta with winkles

SERVES 4

I think the best pasta for this dish is spaghetti. If you're planning to make it yourself, you'll need a pasta machine. This dish is real 'slow food' - you serve the winkles in their shells and need a cocktail stick to remove them. There's no eating this in three seconds flat! I think people are relying too much on convenience foods these days - no-one wants to work for their food by getting fish off the bone or shellfish out of the shell. But the taste is far superior if you are prepared to put in a bit of effort - try a carton of winkles still in their shells from Scarborough Harbour, and you'll see what I mean. Another interesting combination of Italian and Yorkshire produce.

Wash the winkles thoroughly two or three times to make sure all the sand is removed. Fry the onions in the oil until transparent, add the winkles (still in their shells!) and cook for two minutes, then add the garlic and wine. Simmer for a couple of minutes, then add the tomato and fish stock. Allow to reduce for twenty to thirty minutes.

Cook the pasta, drain and add to the winkle sauce, toss the two together and serve immediately.

400g of egg pasta (see page 12)
300g winkles
1 small onion, chopped
2 tsps extra virgin olive oil
1 clove garlic, finely chopped
75ml white wine
1 fresh tomato, chopped
300 ml fish stock (see page 11)

Main

ravioli di cervo e tartufi neri

Venison ravioli with black truffles

SERVES 6

To make this dish, ask your butcher for mixed venison meat - the secondary cuts, like the leg. Don't use the saddle, it's too expensive.

  500g venison, off the bone
  1 onion, quartered
  2 or 3 carrots, scrubbed
  3 sticks celery
  2 cloves garlic, peeled
  1 bayleaf, fresh or dried
  1 sprig fresh rosemary
  2 cloves
  Extra virgin olive oil
  Salt and pepper
  200g cooked spinach
  200g of parmesan cheese, grated
  8 whole eggs
  3 egg yolks
  500g '00' flour
  1 ladleful of beef stock (see page 11)
  Black truffles

Coat the venison, onion, carrots, celery, garlic, bayleaf, rosemary and cloves in a little olive oil, season with salt and pepper, and roast at gas mark 7, 230 degrees C, for sixty to ninety minutes. When cooked, reserve 100g of the venison - this will be used later to make the sauce - add the cooked spinach to the remaining ingredients, remove the cloves, and mince, or chop as finely as possible, the lot. Allow to cool. Add four of the

eggs, beaten, and 150g of the parmesan cheese. Mix together to make a workable paste.

Use the flour and remaining eggs and extra yolks to make the pasta dough (see page 12).

Roll out the dough, and cut into strips approximately 70cm long and 12cm wide. Space teaspoons of the venison stuffing down one side of a strip of pasta, then fold over to cover the stuffing. Seal the ravioli around each teaspoon of venison paste using your fingers, then cut to make little parcels.

To make the sauce, mince the reserved venison and place in a pan with the butter, one ladleful of beef stock and the remaining parmesan, and simmer until thickened to the consistency of double cream.

Bring a pan of water to the boil, and add the ravioli, cooking for approximately four to five minutes.

Place the ravioli in a serving dish, top with the sauce, and garnish with a good helping of shaved black truffle.

Main

trota di mare
con rafano
Sea trout with horseradish

SERVES 4

Sea trout is a much underestimated fish, as good
as salmon any day. It's caught around
Scarborough during the summer, and can be
bought fresh from the water - a real treat! This is
quite a different fish recipe, a Mediterranean
technique with that Yorkshire touch of
horseradish - and not a joint of roast beef in sight!

1 large onion, very finely chopped
4 fillets of sea trout, around 200g each
2 tablespoons extra virgin olive oil
50ml dry white wine
200g whipping cream
Salt and pepper
1 generous tablespoon horseradish sauce

Place the sea trout fillets in a roasting tin with the
onion and olive oil. Bake at gas mark 6, 200
degrees C, for about thirty minutes. Take out of
the oven, and remove the fish, keeping it warm.

Put the roasting tin on the hob, and add to the oil
and onions the wine, salt and pepper, cream and
a generous tablespoon of horseradish sauce. Cook
until the sauce thickens and reduces. Place the
sea trout on a serving dish and top with the
sauce.

gnocchi alla bava
Potato gnocchi with 'dribble'

SERVES 4

There are two different kinds of gnocchi, or dumplings: *gnocchi alla Romana*, which is made with semolina, and *gnocchi alla Piemontese*, which is made with potatoes. You'll need plenty of work space to make gnocchi from scratch, and it is rather time-consuming (you might like to enlist some help from the family) but the end result is worth it! I was shocked the other day to read a recipe in a book by a well-known Italian chef which suggested adding finely chopped sun-dried tomatoes to the basic gnocchi dough. I think this would be a real shame - the delicate flavour of potato gnocchi is so fine that something as tangy and full-flavoured as sun-dried tomatoes would ruin it.

The cheese sauce I like to serve with my gnocchi uses three different cheeses: fontina, which is creamy and mild, and gorgonzola and parmesan, which add bite and richness of flavour.

When I was a child at home, mum making the gnocchi used to be the sign of an upcoming celebration - we used to keep well out of the way. *Alla bava* in the Piemontese dialect literally translates to 'with dribble', because the fontina cheese becomes lovely and runny when it melts. Rachel, my wife, once told my mum that she had made the gnocchi, and I had done the bava, or dribble. Mum thought it was hilarious!

1 kg potatoes
Large knob of butter
300g '00' flour
2 beaten eggs
Pinch of salt
150ml whipping cream
50g gorgonzola cheese
50g fontina cheese
50g parmesan cheese
Large knob of butter
Salt and pepper

Boil the potatoes, and mash with the butter. Then alternately add the flour and eggs, a little at a time, mixing to make a soft dough. Turn the mixture out onto a floured surface, and knead briefly. Cut the dough into four pieces, and roll each piece into a sausage shape. Cut each sausage into small pieces, around 1- 1½ cm long. Press each piece with a fork to make the distinctive gnocchi shape.

Now make the sauce: over a very low heat, melt together in a pan the cream, the three cheeses, the butter and a little salt, until you have a smooth, thick sauce.

Bring a large panful of salted water to the boil, and add the gnocchi. They are cooked when they rise to the surface, which only takes a few minutes. Drain, then add to the sauce, and serve with a generous grinding of black pepper.

Main

orzotto
Barley risotto

SERVES 4

Orzo is the Italian name for barley, one of the grains most commonly-grown in Italy, from where it's exported all over the world for beer-making. It's popular in the North-East, especially the Valtellina region where they use it to make a sort of risotto, using the same technique. This is my version with a Yorkshire flavour: pale ale! The combined flavours of the barley, pancetta and ale is beautiful. I particularly enjoy using Timothy Taylor's Landlord Strong Pale Ale for this recipe.

> 100g butter
> 1 onion, finely chopped
> 200g barley
> 50g minced pork
> 100g pancetta, chopped
> 2 cloves garlic, finely chopped
> 25cl pale ale or bitter
> 1 litre stock (see page 11)
> Salt and pepper

Fry the onion in the butter until golden. Add the pancetta, pork and garlic, and cook briefly. Add the barley, and cook until the butter is absorbed. Add the pale ale or bitter, and salt and pepper, and leave to absorb, stirring from time to time. Keep adding the stock, a little at a time, waiting until each ladleful is absorbed before adding more. The barley will take a little longer to cook than rice, probably between twenty and thirty minutes, although try and keep it *al dente* - don't let it become mushy!

tajarin di meliga

SERVES 4-6

Tajarin di Meliga comes from the Basso Monferrato region. This is a very traditional and typical Piemontese recipe. Usually the tajarin, which are thin strips of pasta, are made just with '00' flour and eggs, but I have replaced some of the flour with meliga, or polenta, which I think gives the finished product a most beautiful colour.

> 650g '00' flour
> 350g maize (polenta) flour
> 8 whole eggs
> 6 egg yolks
> 300g chicken livers, chopped
> 1 onion, finely chopped
> 50g pancetta or streaky bacon, chopped
> 2 tablespoons of extra virgin olive oil
> 3 tablespoons of tomato puree
> 50ml dry white wine
> Salt and pepper

To make the tajarin, sieve together the two flours, and add the beaten eggs. Mix together to form a stiffish dough, roll out and cut into fine ribbons around 1/4cm wide. Cook in boiling water for two to three minutes.

Meanwhile, make the sauce. Fry the onions in the olive oil until transparent, then add the pancetta or bacon. Fry for five minutes, then add the chicken livers, tomato puree and salt and pepper. Stir together, then add the white wine. Reduce slightly, until the sauce is the consistency of double cream. Serve on top of the tajarin.

risotto con seppia e tartufi neri

Risotto with cuttlefish and truffles

SERVES 4

This is another dish using fine Scarborough produce and Piemontese truffles. It's best to use black truffles for this dish, but if you can't find them, look out for the truffle-flavoured rice you can sometimes find in Italian delicatessens. Or, if you're a real truffle fan, use both!

Cuttlefish isn't widely used in this country, but it's delicious - a little like squid, but rather more tender, and with a much meatier texture. I like to use small cuttlefish, about 3cm long, using both the head and the body. To clean the fish, take off all the skin, and remove the long, single bone from inside. Or you could always ask your fishmonger to do this for you!

Have the stock hot and ready to use. Fry the onion in the oil until transparent. Add the cuttlefish, and cook for a few minutes. Add the rice, and stir until coated in oil. Add the white wine and garlic and season with salt and pepper. When the wine is absorbed, add the stock, a ladle at a time, allowing each ladleful to become absorbed before you add the next. When the rice is nicely *al dente*, but not mushy, take the pan off the heat and stir in the butter until it is melted. Serve with the finely shaved truffle on top.

2 tablespoons extra virgin olive oil
Half an onion, finely chopped
500g cuttlefish, cleaned weight, chopped
400g rice (arborio, carnaroli or vialone nano)
125ml dry white wine
1 clove garlic, finely chopped
Salt and pepper
1 litre fish stock (see page 11)
1 large knob of butter
Black truffle

Main

calamari con la zucca
Squid stuffed with pumpkin

SERVES 6

I love to cook with the tender baby squid which
you can buy at Scarborough Harbour in the
autumn, which is also when pumpkin is at its
best. I prefer not to use squid any larger than
about 10cm for this dish - any bigger, and I think
they're really only fit for boiling and braising.
These tiny beasts only need cleaning and can then
be cooked straight away without any pre-boiling.

  12 baby, or very small, squid
  200g pumpkin, finely diced
  1 small onion, finely chopped
  Salt and pepper
  1 tablespoon extra virgin olive oil
  1 large knob of butter
  2 cloves garlic, finely chopped
  125ml dry white wine

Clean the squid and detach the tentacles from the
body (or get your fishmonger to do this for you).
Fry the tentacles, pumpkin, onion and a pinch of
salt and pepper with half the oil for just a few
minutes. When cooked, chop the mixture
coarsely and stuff into the bodies of the squid,
securing the openings with cocktail sticks.

Place the stuffed squid into a saucepan with the
remaining oil, butter, garlic and white wine.
Cook for ten minutes, and don't forget to remove
the cocktail sticks before serving - or at least warn
your guests if you're planning to leave them in!

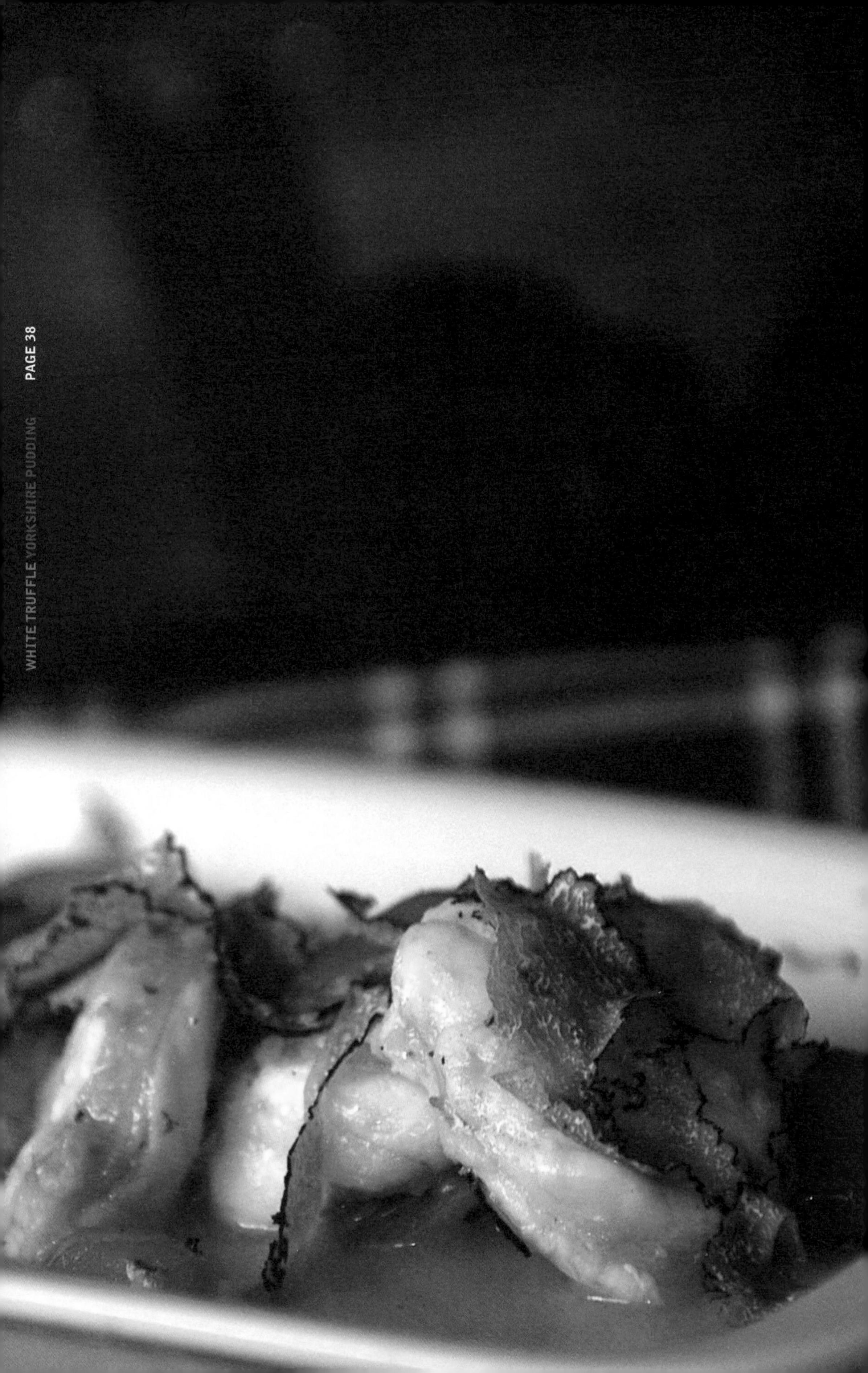

zuppa di coda di rospo al tartufo

Monkfish stew with truffles

SERVES 6

You can use either white or black truffles for this, depending on what you can afford and what you can find (white truffles are in season between October and December; you can find black truffles nearly all year round). Black truffle butter is much cheaper, and easy to cook with.

1kg monkfish, or other firm white fish
12 cherry tomatoes, quartered
1 teaspoon garlic, finely chopped
2 tablespoons extra virgin olive oil
125ml dry white wine
1 whole fresh truffle or 1 generous tablespoon of truffle butter

Heat the olive oil until it starts to lightly smoke, then add the fish and fry until it is golden on each side. Add the cherry tomatoes and cook for two to three more minutes, then add the white wine and the chopped garlic. Cook, stirring gently, until the tomato juices and wine thicken and form a sauce. If you're using a fresh truffle, serve the dish and shave the truffle over. If you're using truffle butter, stir into the sauce at the last minute, then take off the heat.

risotto in bianco con tartufo

Risotto with white truffles

SERVES 4

Risotto in bianco means literally 'risotto cooked in white', or completely plain, and you could serve this dish without the truffles and still have a classic, simple and delicious dish. There are three types of rice usually used for risotti: arborio, carnaroli and vialone nano. Which you choose is down to personal preference - for this recipe, I prefer arborio, because it's a little 'chubbier' than the others. The final touch of taking the dish off the heat and stirring through butter and parmesan cheese is called *mantecare*, and adds a touch of luxury to what is essentially a simple and straightforward dish. This is the only risotto which really brings out the full truffle flavour.

Fry the onions in the olive oil until transparent. Add the rice and stir until the oil and onion juices are absorbed, then slowly add the white wine, and cook, stirring regularly, until absorbed. Add the stock, a ladleful at a time, until absorbed and the rice is cooked *al dente*. This should take fifteen to twenty minutes, depending on which rice you are using. Season to taste with the salt and pepper. Take off the heat, and add the butter and parmesan, stirring until creamy. Serve topped with generous shavings of white truffle.

1 medium white onion, finely chopped
50ml extra virgin olive oil
400g arborio rice
125ml glass dry white wine
1 litre beef stock (see page 11)
1 large knob butter
A handful, around 50g, grated parmesan cheese
Salt and pepper
White truffle

Main

rombo al forno
Baked turbot

SERVES 4

Living by the seaside, it's possible to get hold of
whole turbot, rather than just the fillet.
Sometimes you can buy whole baby turbot,
weighing around 500g each, which are
particularly good for this dish. This is a nice
earthy meal for autumn or winter, with gorgeous
truffly mashed potato, which looks very
impressive.

  4 turbot around 500g each, cleaned
  600g old potatoes
  100g butter
  125ml milk
  Pinch of tarragon
  Salt and pepper
  Black truffles to garnish

Place the turbot on a lightly oiled baking tray and
bake at gas mark 6, 200 degrees C, for eight to ten
minutes. Meanwhile, boil the potatoes, and mash
them with the butter, milk, tarragon, salt and
pepper.

Serve the turbot with the mashed potato to the
side, garnished with chopped (not sliced) black
truffle.

stufato di pesce di scarborough

Scarborough fish stew

SERVES 4

This dish uses some of the wonderful fish you can buy in Scarborough during the summer months. You may find it hard to get hold of fresh scampi, as much of the catch that is landed here is quickly sold abroad or to Scotland. Ask your fishmonger to find some for you, or go straight to the harbour. Use medium-sized Dover sole: the meat is more delicate, and it's also more cost-effective, as the price per kilo goes up the larger the fish is. Red mullet is also very good in the summer. Again, try and use medium-sized fish, probably around 300g each. If your fishmonger fillets the fish for you, ask him for the bones to make stock, and also use the heads of the scampi.

If you are lucky enough to grow your own courgettes, or know someone who does, hang on to the flowers for this recipe. You do occasionally see them in the shops as well.

1 carrot, finely chopped
1 onion, finely chopped
4 tbsp extra virgin olive oil
50ml dry white wine
25ml brandy
Salt and pepper
1 litre fish stock (see page 11)
6 cherry tomatoes, chopped
6 courgette flowers
8 fresh scampi
Fillets from 2 medium Dover soles
Fillets from 2 medium red mullet
Large bunch of Italian flat leaf parsley

Fry the carrot and onion in half the oil until tender, then add the white wine, brandy, salt and pepper and all but a ladleful of the fish stock. Allow to reduce a little, then add the cherry tomatoes and the courgette flowers and cook for another eight to ten minutes.

In another pan, sauté the scampi tails and fillets of Dover sole and red mullet in the rest of the oil until they begin to lose their transparency - a matter of seconds. Add a ladle of fish stock and cook for a further three to four minutes. Place the carrot, onions, tomatoes and courgette flowers on a serving dish, top with the fish pieces and garnish with a nice big bunch of Italian flat leaf parsley

fritto misto di mare
Mixed fried fish

SERVES 4

In my home town of Moncalvo in northern Italy, this dish would be made with a mixture of meats and vegetables, ox being the most popular. But I have adapted this to give it a Scarborough feel, using many of the wonderful species of fresh fish I can buy at the Harbour - some common, some not so well-known! You can, of course, substitute your own favourite varieties of white fish.

As always, try to use the best free range eggs you can find - better nutritionally, and they also give a much better colour to the dish. I like to serve this on white china to show off the wonderful golden colour. This also makes a lovely antipasto dish.

Ingredients
100g each of: bleg (pouting), ling, monkfish, red mullet, squid, Scarborough woof, soft white roe
1 head of broccoli, cut into florets and blanched
1 aubergine, sliced into discs approx $1/2$ cm thick
1 leek, sliced lengthwise in to strips
1 courgette, sliced into discs approx $1/2$ cm thick
6 eggs
1 tablespoon of minced garlic
Salt and pepper
50cl whipping cream
400g white breadcrumbs
2 pinches of finely chopped parsley
1 litre of sunflower oil, for shallow frying
1 tablespoon of English mustard
4 tablespoon olive oil
1 egg yolk
Juice of $1/2$ lemon
Salt and pepper

Cut all the fish into bite-sized chunks of roughly the same size - this will help them to cook uniformly. Beat together the eggs, garlic, salt, pepper and cream to make a wash, and in a separate dish, mix together the breadcrumbs and parsley. Dip the fish pieces and vegetable slices into the egg wash, then into the breadcrumb mix. Shallow fry each breadcrumbed piece in the sunflower oil for a few minutes each side, or until golden.
To make the sauce, beat together the mustard, olive oil, egg yolk; lemon juice and salt and pepper. Serve on the side of the plate as a dip.

Main

astice con pesche gialle
Lobster with peaches

SERVES 2

I love to serve fish with fresh fruit - it gives it a real twist! Ask your fishmonger for a local lobster- they're exported all over the place, but always taste best when they're eaten close to home.

  2 600g live lobsters
  2 tablespoons of olive oil
  3 yellow peaches
  50g butter
  Juice of $1/2$ lemon
  1 tablespoon balsamic vinegar
  25ml Sambuca
  Salt and pepper

Boil the lobsters for twenty minutes. When cooked, remove the lobsters from the pan and clean, but keep the water for the stock. Alternatively, buy a pre-cooked lobster, and use 100ml of fish stock.

Cut the lobster into pieces, and sauté in the olive oil for a few minutes.

Blanch the peaches in boiling water and remove the skin and stones. Liquidize the flesh of two of the peaches.

In another pan, briefly fry together the peach purée and the butter, then add the lemon juice, balsamic vinegar, Sambuca, lobster stock and salt and pepper. Simmer until reduced.

Spoon the sauce onto a serving plate, and arrange the pieces of lobster on top. Slice the whole peach, and use to decorate.

anguilla al barolo
Eel in red wine

SERVES 4

People can be put off by the thought of eating eel, but it's a tasty, meaty fish, and quite delicious when cooked with a full-bodied red wine such as Barolo. You could always use a nice Barbera as an alternative. Eels are fished around the Humber, a tradition which started because there's a large Dutch community in this area. Many of the eels are exported to Holland.

  1 kg cleaned eels
  $1/2$ litre of Barolo wine
  1 sprig parsley, chopped
  $1/2$ onion, finely chopped
  1 carrot, diced
  $1/2$ kg arborio rice
  Pinch of salt
  Knob of butter
  50g parmesan cheese, grated

Cut the eel into pieces, and place in a saucepan with the wine, parsley, onion and carrots. Leave to simmer over a low flame for around thirty minutes. Meanwhile, boil the rice in salted water for twenty minutes, then drain and sauté with the butter and parmesan cheese - it will become very creamy. Place on a serving plate, and put the eel on top.

Main

luccio ai funghi
Pike with mushrooms

SERVES 4

This delicious dish uses pike, the largest freshwater predator, and a very tasty white fish. I think it's a good idea to start using more freshwater fish, especially as the quotas on catching sea fish are becoming increasingly restrictive. As a child, I lived near the River Po, and we would eat freshwater fish regularly. However, if you find it difficult to get hold of pike, try Scarborough woof instead - it's still delicious!

150g fresh champignon or porcini mushrooms
1kg (cleaned weight) pike, cleaned and filleted
40g butter
50ml glass of dry white wine
50g plain flour
1 tablespoon whipping cream

If you are using fresh porcini mushrooms, slice them then soften in hot water for about thirty minutes, then drain. Champignon mushrooms simply need slicing. Melt half the butter in a saucepan and saute the mushrooms for around twenty minutes, then add the white wine. Allow the wine to reduce, then sprinkle the mushrooms with flour, and leave to cool. Meanwhile, cut the fillets of pike into thin slices, and fry in the rest of the butter for a few minutes. Place the fillets in a well-greased baking dish, mix the mushroom mixture with the cream, and pour over. Bake in the oven at gas mark 8, 230 degrees C, for about ten minutes.

Main

pollo farcito
Stuffed chicken

SERVES 4

You may want to ask your butcher to bone the chicken for you!

1 chicken, boned
6 sprigs fresh rosemary
200g boiled ham
4 tablespoons olive oil
Salt and pepper

Fill the chicken cavity: stuff it with a little of the ham, then a rosemary sprig, then more ham, continuing until four of the sprigs have been used. Place in a roasting tin, drizzle with the oil and sprinkle with salt and pepper. Add the remaining two sprigs of rosemary to the tin, and cover. Roast at gas mark 7, 220 degrees C, for approximately forty minutes, or until the chicken juices run clear when pierced with a skewer. Slice the chicken into slices approximately 1cm thick. Eat hot or cold.

pollo alla bella rosin
Chicken La Bella Rosin

SERVES 4

La Bella Rosin was a poor but beautiful girl who lived in Moncalvo. When the King of Italy visited the city, he fell in love with her. They married, but she always stayed close to her Moncalvese roots. This dish celebrates her, combining a 'poor' food - chicken - with a rich sauce.

You could use Parma ham for this, but it seems a shame to cook it. Instead, use good old-fashioned Yorkshire ham - it's just as good!

Use young, tender sprigs of rosemary for this dish that way, you can eat both the leaves and the stem.

4 chicken breasts
100ml cream
2 sprigs fresh rosemary
2 cloves garlic, finely chopped
50ml chicken stock
100g cured Yorkshire ham, cut into ribbons
50g parmesan cheese, thickly sliced

Grill the chicken breasts until cooked. Meanwhile, make the sauce. Place all the other ingredients except the parmesan cheese, into a saucepan, stir together, and place over a medium heat. Allow to simmer until you have a sauce the consistency of double cream.
Place the chicken breasts on a plate and pour over the sauce. Place several slices of parmesan on each chicken breast.

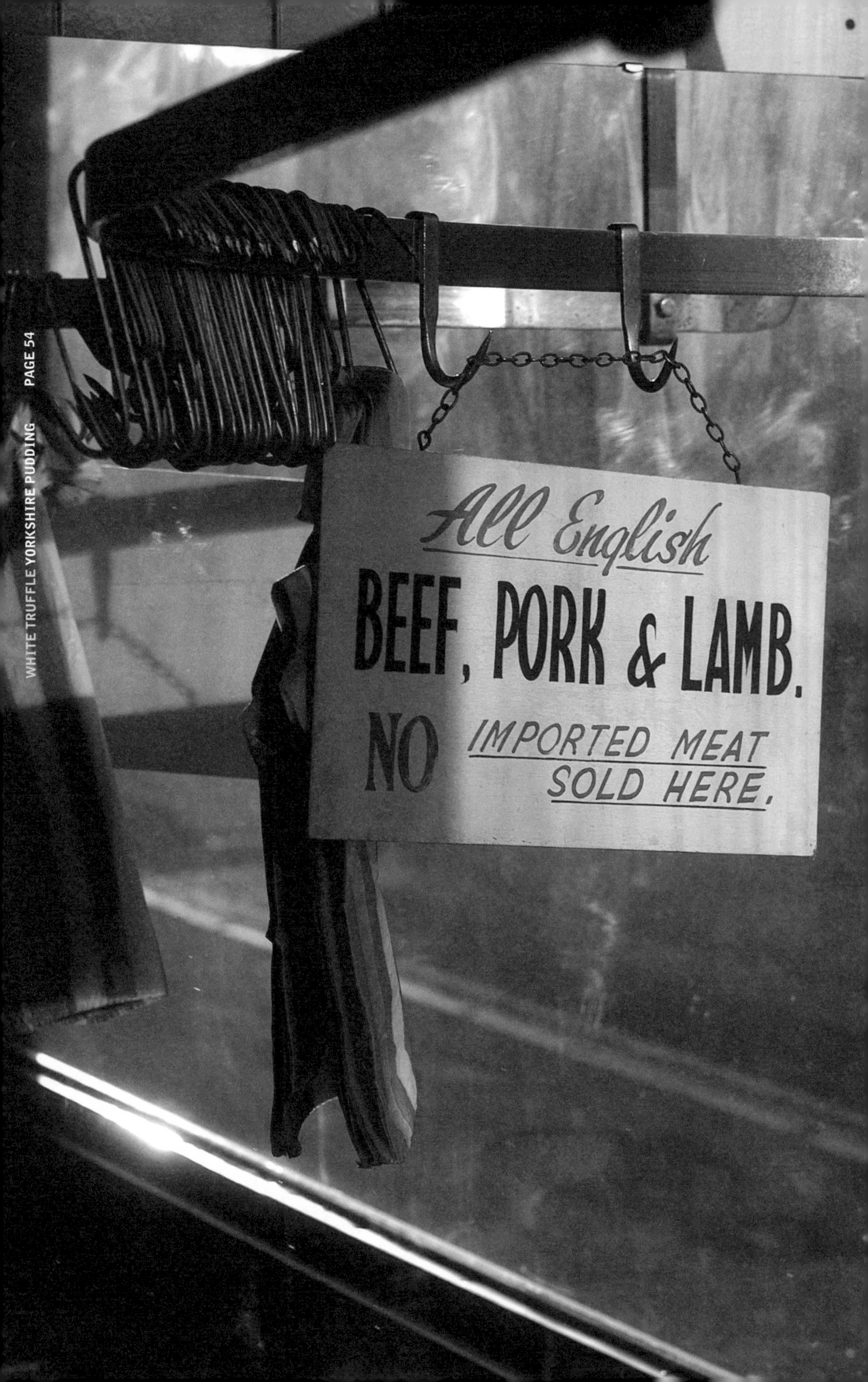
All English
BEEF, PORK & LAMB.
NO IMPORTED MEAT
SOLD HERE.

Main

filetto alla piemontese
Fillet steak Piemontese-style

SERVES 4

This dish really must be served rare, or blue, to get the true taste!

    8 2oz medallions of beef fillet
    '00' flour to dust
    Knob of butter
    1 teaspoon finely chopped garlic
    Salt and pepper
    60ml dry white wine
    1 small bunch flat leaf parsley, chopped

Dust the medallions of beef with the flour.
Put the butter in a pan and melt until it bubbles - don't allow it to smoke. Add the fillet to the pan and fry for a few seconds each side. Add the salt, pepper and garlic and cook for a few seconds more - don't burn the garlic as this will make the dish taste bitter! Add the white wine and cook until the sauce starts to thicken.

Serve sprinkled with the chopped parsley.

trippa
Tripe

SERVES 4

This is a lovely old-fashioned recipe for an old - fashioned ingredient: tripe. It's increasingly difficult to track down, but good butchers should stock it. And ideally, of course, that's where you should be buying all your meat!
The tripe in Britain is a little different to that we have in Italy. I find that British tripe is washed too many times, and becomes more jelly-like than meaty. Ask your butcher if he can order you a nice fresh, unbleached piece.
This dish is a particular favourite of Rachel's. When we go to Italy, she always puts in a special request to my mum, as she makes this beautifully.

    600g tripe
    1/2 onion
    70g lard
    Knob of butter
    2 cloves garlic, finely chopped
    Salt and pepper
    Nutmeg, grated
    1 litre beef stock
    Parmesan cheese

Cut the tripe into 1cm strips, slice the onion finely, and fry together in the lard until the onions are transparent. Add the garlic and butter, and simmer for a few minutes. Season with salt, pepper and nutmeg, and then slowly add the stock. Leave to simmer over a low heat for seven to eight hours.

Before serving, dust with grated parmesan cheese, and serve with bread fried in olive oil.

stracotto di coda di manzo e ceci

Chickpea and oxtail stew

SERVES 6

This is a satisfying, wintry kind of a dish. *Stracotto* means "over-cooked", and that's what this dish is! Mashing the dish at the end helps it to thicken, and gives it a wonderfully rib-sticking consistency.

For the frugal amongst you, here's a great way of using up those bits of parmesan rind that you might normally throw away: keep all your rinds (you can freeze them) and, when you make this dish, cut them into tiny squa res (discarding any bits with print on them) and add to the stew five minutes from the end. The result is deliciously chewy, cheesey morsels which really add something special to this dish. Parmesan is especially high in calcium, and it's particularly concentrated in the rind. When I was little - they don't do it now - Italians used to keep the rind for the toddlers. They made a hole in the rind and hung it round our necks on a ribbon. We would chew it - good for our teeth, and kept us occupied!

The flavour of this dish is best if you use dried chickpeas, rather than tinned. Soak them in cold water for at least twelve hours before using, then drain and rinse.

1 onion, finely chopped
Knob of butter
2 tablespoons of extra virgin olive oil
1 oxtail, jointed
'00' flour to dust
Beef stock (see page 11)
2 cloves of garlic, coarsely chopped
500g chickpeas
200g old potatoes, diced
1 sprig rosemary

Fry the onion in the butter and olive oil until transparent. Dust the oxtail with the flour and add to the pan, cooking the pieces until they are golden all over. Add the stock and simmer for about one hour. Add the garlic and the chick peas, then simmer for around another sixty to ninety minutes. By this time, the meat on the oxtail pieces should come easily away from the bone; remove all the pieces and strip off the meat, adding it back into the pan, and discard the bones. Add the potatoes and rosemary, and simmer for another twenty minutes and then, using a potato masher, roughly mash the stew. Serve topped with crispy fried croutons.

Main

lingua di bue
Ox tongue with parsley sauce

SERVES 4

People still buy cured ox tongue in tins and serve it cold, but it's rare to start from scratch with a raw tongue in all its glory! Do try this - it's a very lean meat, and absolutely delicious. And you can use the stock that's left over from this dish for wonderful soups, risotti, or for braising meats. People can be put off by the idea of using offal: a man once asked us how we could possibly eat something that came from an animal's mouth - and then he ate eggs!

1 fresh ox tongue

2 carrots

1 onion

2 sticks celery

2 bay leaves

300g fresh flat leaf parsley, roughly chopped

100ml extra virgin olive oil

4 tinned tomatoes, chopped

Pinch sugar

Salt and pepper

1 hot red chilli

Bring a pan with four to five litres of water to the boil, and simmer the tongue with the carrots, onion, celery, bay leaves and salt and pepper for three to three-and-a-half hours.

To make the sauce, which is called *Bagnetto Verde*, mix together the oil, parsley, tomatoes, sugar, chilli and a pinch each of salt and pepper. Use a little extra oil if necessary. Allow the flavours to mingle for at least two hours.

Drain the tongue and slice into slices about 1cm thick. Serve warm with the *Bagnetto Verde* on the side.

beccaccia con crostone
Woodcock with crusty polenta

SERVES 4

Game is plentiful in this region, and sadly underused. Woodcock is a delicious bird, a little larger than a pigeon: you can find it in the autumn in good butchers, or, if you're lucky enough to know one, get it directly from the hunter! I was delighted to find it in this country - I hadn't seen it in Italy for many years. Watch out for the fine bones when you eat it.

4 cleaned woodcock
8 slices pancetta or bacon
Knob of butter
1 slice cooked ham, cut into thin strips
1/2 carrot, scraped
1 stick of celery, chopped
2 pinches chopped parsley
1 bay leaf
1/2 litre chicken stock
50ml glass Marsala wine
250g polenta

Wrap each woodcock in two slices of the pancetta or bacon, and tie with string into a roll shape. In a casserole dish, melt the butter then saute the ham, carrot, celery, parsley and bayleaf for a few minutes. Add the woodcock, together with the stock and marsala, and simmer for twenty-five to thirty-five minutes.

Meanwhile, make the polenta. Bring one litre of water to the boil and gradually add the polenta, stirring all the while, until thickened to the consistency of mashed potato. Take off the heat, and, when cool enough to handle, turn out onto a work surface, roll out to around 1-1 1/2 cm thick and cut into rough slices. Grill or oven bake until crusty.

When the woodcock is cooked, remove it from the pan and keep warm. Mash all the remaining ingredients to make a thick sauce. Place the polenta on a plate, top with the woodcock, and pour over the sauce.

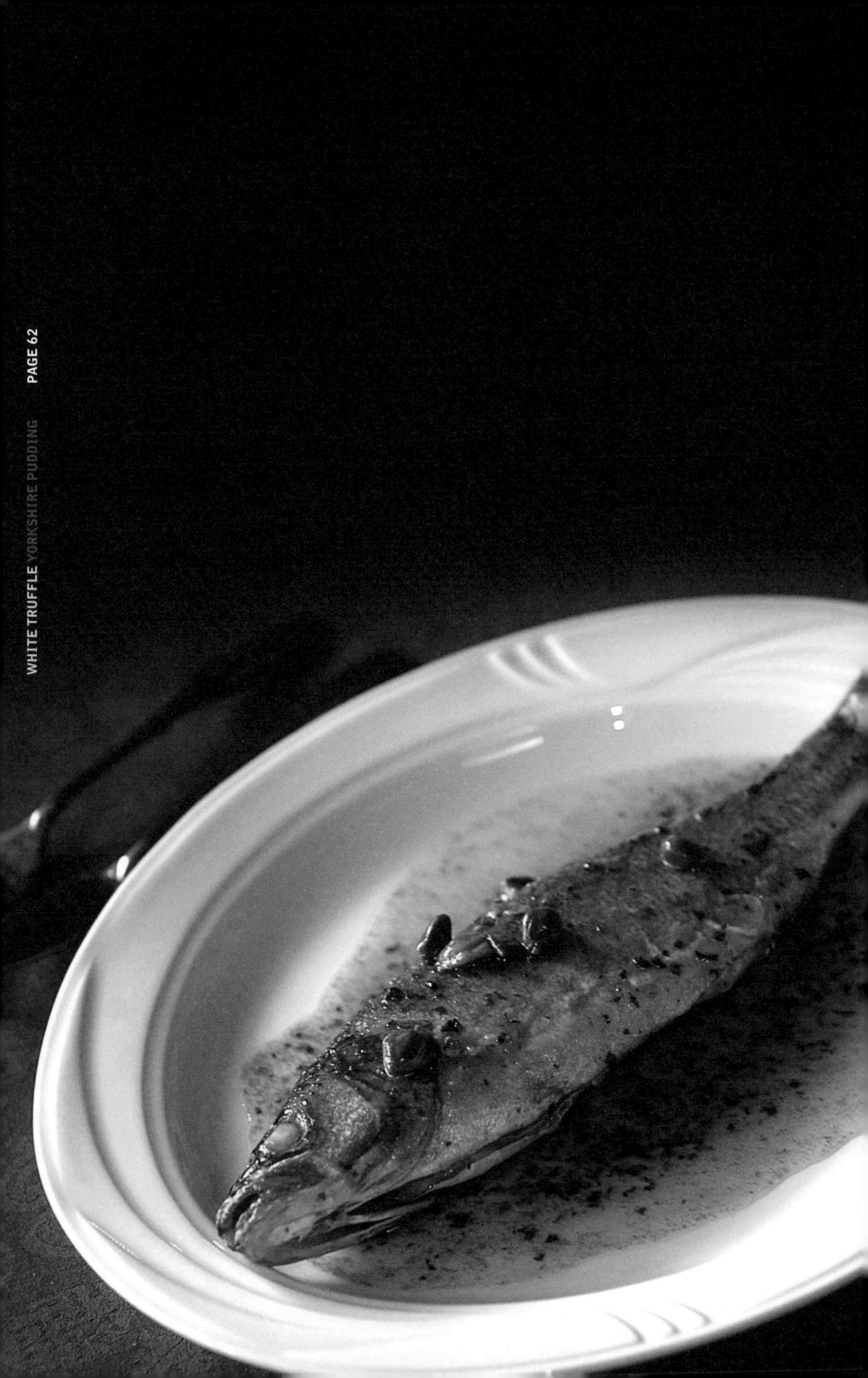

branzino del mulino
Sea bass of the mill

SERVES 4

This is a lovely springtime dish made with sea
bass; you can also use red mullet. Make sure the
fish is clean inside, and carefully remove the
scales from the outside using a small knife - or get
your fishmonger to do this! If you see any Italian
recipe which includes the words *del Mulino*, or 'of
the mill', you can assume it will involve flour.

  4 sea bass, around 250g each
  Pinch of marjoram
  Salt and pepper
  Milk to coat
  Plain flour to dust
  2 knobs of butter
  6 capers
  Juice of 1/2 lemon
  2 pinches parsley, chopped

Fill the cavity of the fish with the marjoram, and
season inside with salt and pepper. Pour the milk
over the fish, then sprinkle with flour. Melt one
of the knobs of butter in a pan, and fry each side
of the fish for a few minutes. Remove the fish
and put to one side, keeping warm, reserving the
juices in the pan. Add to them the capers, lemon
juice and the second knob of butter and cook
together, stirring occasionally, until the sauce
becomes the consistency of whipping cream. Stir
in the chopped parsley, place the fish on a serving
dish, and pour the sauce over. This is lovely
served with boiled baby new potatoes.

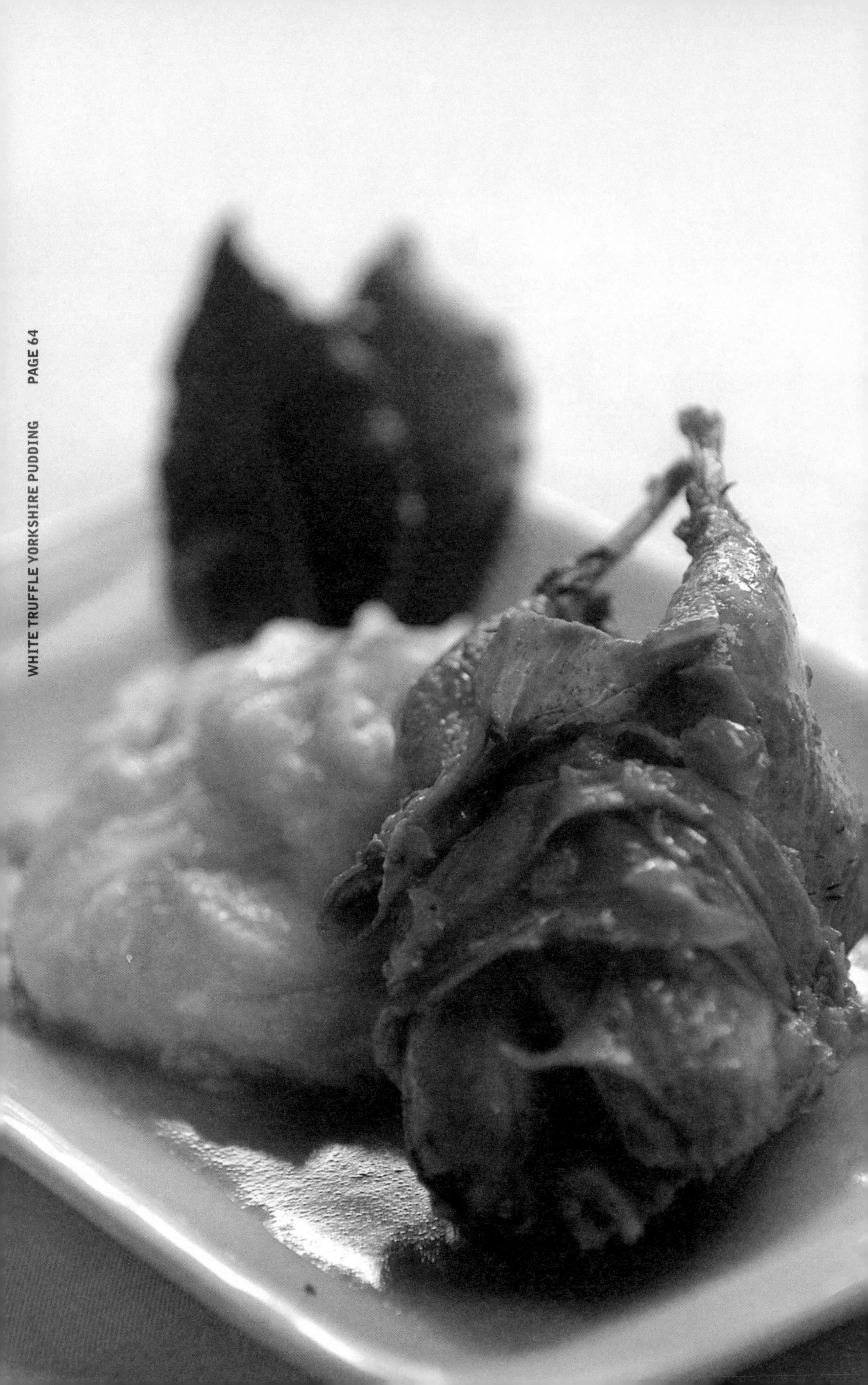

pernice al tartufo nero
Partridge with black truffles

SERVES 4

A lot of people in this country don't like the taste of game, finding it too strong. But that's because game in this country is hung with the guts still in. In Italy, any game - we call it *pelo* and *piuma,* or skin and feathers - is cleaned before being left in the fridge for a week. The meat is still tenderized, a process we call *frollare*, but it doesn't get that very strong, gamey flavour which you get over here.

- 4 partridges, cleaned
- 4 large slices of Parma ham, cut thick
- 1 medium onion, coarsely chopped
- 2 cloves
- 2 bay leaves, fresh or dried
- 2 tablespoons olive oil
- Salt and pepper
- 250ml chicken stock (see page 11)
- 2 black truffles

Pigeon with black truffles is a classic recipe in Italy, but I like to use the partridge which is abundant round here, and is in season at the same time as the truffles.

Wrap the partridges in the Parma ham. Fry the onions in the oil, then add the cloves and the bay leaves. When the onions become transparent, add the partridge and brown all over. Add a couple of ladles of stock, season with the salt and pepper, cover and cook on a medium heat for around twenty minutes. Finely shave one of the truffles directly into the pan and stir through the sauce. Place the partridge on a serving dish with the juices, removing the cloves and bay leaves and finely shave the second truffle over it. Serve with polenta.

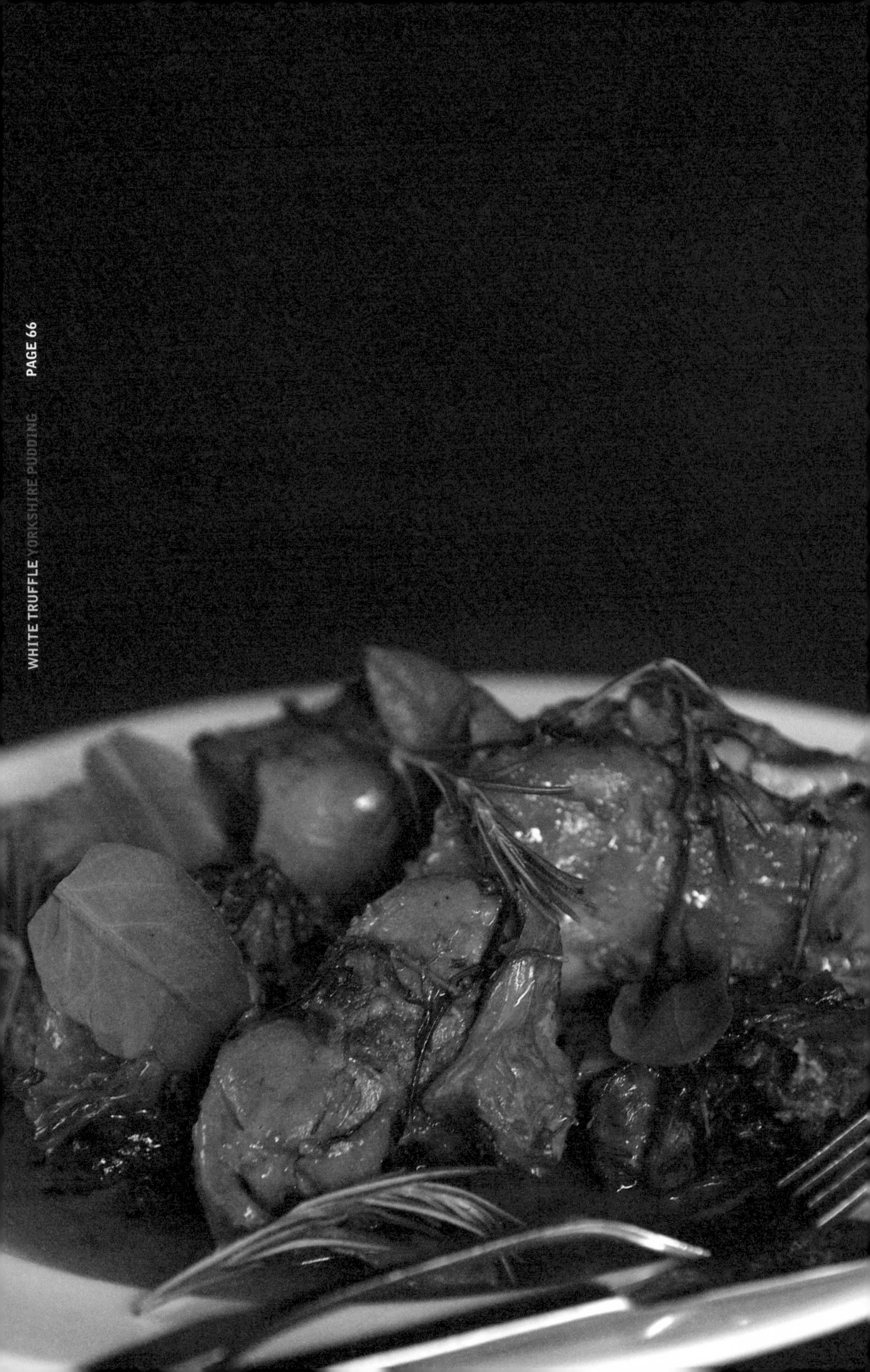

Main

coniglio in padella
Rabbit in the pan

SERVES 4

It's important to use a farmed, rather than a wild, rabbit for this, as the flavour is milder - your butcher should be able to get you one. And ask him to joint it for you!

  Extra virgin olive oil
  1 farmed rabbit, jointed
  125ml dry white wine
  1 clove garlic, sliced
  2 sprigs rosemary
  Salt and pepper
  3 cloves
  2 bay leaves, fresh or dried
  1/2 litre chicken stock

Put enough oil in a pan to just coat the bottom and heat to a light haze, then add the rabbit pieces and fry gently on each side for about ten minutes, or until brown.

Add the white wine, rosemary, garlic, salt and pepper, cloves and bay leaves and simmer until most of the liquid has reduced. Add the stock, a little at a time, and simmer until the rabbit is cooked. This could take up to forty minutes depending on the thickness of the cut of rabbit. Place the rabbit pieces on a plate and pour over enough of the pan juices to lightly glaze it.

Serve on its own or with polenta concia.

polenta concia

SERVES 4 TO 6

This is a traditional recipe - using just fontina. You could, however, add 30g of fresh gorgonzola if you like the rich flavour. Do not use hard gorgonzola, which is not the real thing. Go to a good delicatessen where they should stock the creamy stuff - the flavour will be much better!

  250g polenta
  1 litre water
  100g fontina, cut into thick slices
  Pinch salt

Add the polenta to the boiling salted water, and stir continuously for twenty to thirty minutes, or until it is the consistency of mashed potato. Place a quarter of the mix into a serving dish, then add a layer of cheese, repeating until all the polenta and cheese is used up. The heat of the polenta will melt the cheese.

This dish can be eaten on its own or served with stews, and is perfect with the rabbit dish.

pacchetti di fagiano fritti

Shallow-fried parcels of pheasant

SERVES 6-8

500g of cleaned and boned pheasant

2 medium carrots, scraped

3 sticks of celery

1 medium onion, peeled

2 cloves of garlic

4 cloves

125ml red wine

Salt and pepper

50g parmesan cheese, grated

4 eggs, beaten

500g fresh pasta (see page 12)

100g minced pork

Knob of butter

1 litre chicken stock (see page 11)

20g parmesan cheese, shaved

1 litre vegetable oil

To make the sauce, fry the minced pork in the butter, then add the chicken stock. Simmer for around thirty minutes until you have a light sauce. In a pan, heat a couple of inches of oil to a light haze, then fry the parcels of pasta for a few minutes. Drain on kitchen paper. You will probably need to do this in batches.

When all the parcels are fried, place in a serving bowl, pour over the sauce, and add the shavings of parmesan.

Place the pheasant, all the vegetables, garlic, cloves and wine into a roasting dish, cover, and roast at gas mark 9, 240 degrees C, for one hour. Allow to cool.

Make the pasta (see page 12) and cut into sheets approximately 8cm long and 4cm wide. Season the cooled pheasant mixture with the salt and pepper, remove the cloves, then mince. Stir in the grated parmesan and eggs to make a moist, but not soggy, paste, then use to make ravioli parcels (see page 27 for technique).

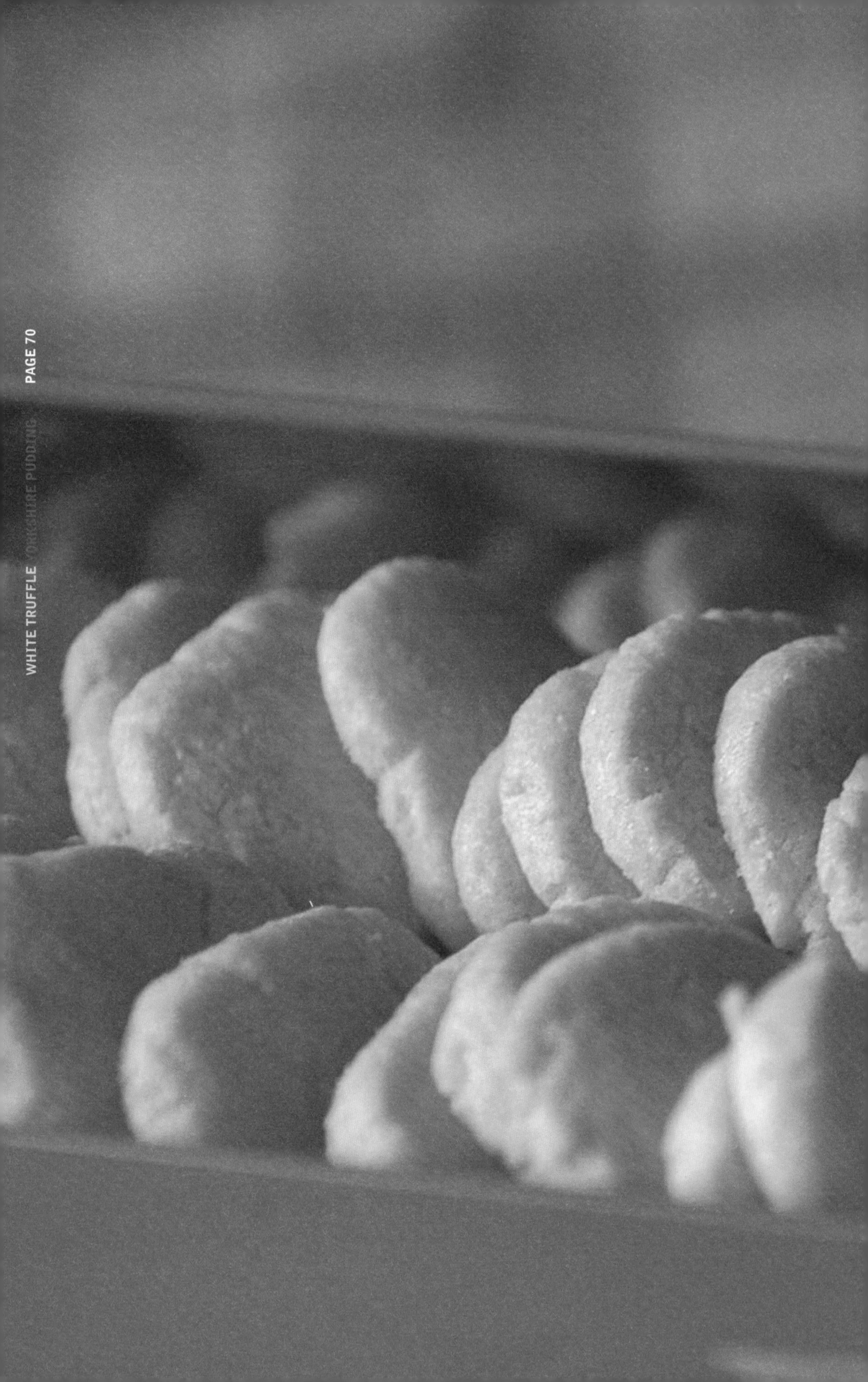

Pudding

crema di torrone
Nougat cream

SERVES 4

Crema di torrone is simply whipped cream and nougat. This reminds me of fairs in Italy when I was a child: there were always big chunks of gorgeous nougat to be had around festival time. These days, you can buy all sorts of variations, but when I was little, it was always hard nougat, and my father used to break it up for my brother, my sister and me with a little hammer. We used to chew it for hours to keep the taste!

This cream can be served with many of the other desserts in this recipe book. You'll be surprised at just how nutty it tastes. It's lovely on its own, just sprinkled with toasted hazelnut, or beautifully compliments many other sweets, even ice creams or tiramisu.

The best way to chop the nougat is to freeze it for several hours until it becomes very brittle, and then run it through a blender.

    100ml cream, whipped
    100g nougat, finely chopped
    6 extra toasted hazelnuts (optional)

Whip the cream until stiff, and then fold in the nougat powder. Chop the toasted hazelnuts, if using, and sprinkle on top.

bicciolani di vercelli
Vercelli biscuits

MAKES 30-40

Vercelli is one of the first towns in the Pianura Padana, or Padana Valley, which is famous for both its rice cultivation, and for the maize flour used in this recipe. Eat these with any of the other sweets in this book, or on their own with coffee.

    200g unsalted butter
    200g caster sugar
    200g polenta, or maize flour
    300g '00' flour
    3 egg yolks, beaten

Cream together the butter and sugar. Sift in the maize flour, '00' flour and add the eggs, then mix to a firm dough. Leave to rest for four to five hours. Then shape the dough into a large sausage and slice into small, disc-shaped biscuits. Place on a greased baking tray, and bake at gas mark 4, 180 degrees C, for twenty to twenty-five minutes, or until pale golden in colour.

Pudding

bunèt

Piemontese dark chocolate dessert

SERVES 6

This is a simple way to make bunèt, a classic Piemontese pudding.

75g good quality cocoa powder
75g caster sugar
75g amaretti biscuits
600ml whipping cream
1 tablespoon gelatine powder

Mix the cocoa powder and sugar together.

In another dish, crush the amaretti biscuits quite coarsely.

Simmer the cream for a couple of minutes, then bring to the boil and take off the heat.

In a dish, dissolve the gelatine in a couple of tablespoons of warm water. Add the gelatine and cocoa mixture to the cream and whisk quite briskly until it is mixed together well. Allow the cream to cool to tepid, whisking two or three times more as it does. Fold in the crushed amaretti biscuits, then pour into ramekins. Allow to cool completely and then refrigerate.

Turn out on to a plate to serve, with a little whipped cream and perhaps a whole amaretto biscuit.

macedonia di frutta con le noci e maraschino

Piemontese fruit salad

SERVES 4

This is a very colourful summer dessert, delicious with ice cream. In Piemonte, we eat lots of nuts, and I always add them to fruit salads - either hazelnuts or my favourite, walnuts.

2 yellow peaches, skinned and diced
1 canteloupe melon, balled
200g strawberries, quartered
200g cherries, stoned and halved
100g blueberries
100g blackberries
2 kiwi fruit, diced
2 plums, diced
100g raspberries
100g walnuts, broken
Juice of 1 lemon
1 tablespoon sugar
125ml glass maraschino liquer

Try to dice all the larger fruits into chunks of roughly the same size. Put all the fruit and the walnuts into a large bowl, and sprinkle with the sugar, lemon juice, and maraschino. Gently fold through, taking care not to bruise or mash the fruit.

Cover and leave in the fridge to marinate for at least one hour before serving.

Pudding

torta di formaggio alle pesche con crosta di amaretti

Peach cheesecake with an amaretti crust

SERVES 6-8

Ricotta is a mild-tasting sheep's cheese, incredibly versatile for both sweet and savoury recipes. In the south of Italy, they like to salt it, bake it until it's almost dry, and then grate it over pasta, as well as using it in sweet dishes. When I was a child growing up in Moncalvo, the shepherds used to bring their herds down from the mountains for the winter, and we would buy the ricotta so fresh, it was still warm! My mother used to mix it with sugar, and we'd have it for breakfast - what a treat that was! You can recreate the taste by stirring a generous tablespoon of caster sugar through a 200g tub of ricotta, perfect as a pudding in its own right.

70g butter, melted
100g digestive biscuits, crushed
50g amaretti biscuits, finely crushed
1 tablespoon powdered gelatine
1 egg, separated
100g ricotta cheese
50g caster sugar
300ml whipping cream
3 large ripe yellow peaches, 2 very finely chopped,1 sliced for decoration
2 tablespoons peach jam

Mix the butter and biscuit mixture together with a spoon. Press the mixture into a loose - bottomed cake tin (approx. 20 cm diameter).

In a bowl, sprinkle the gelatine into 45 ml warm water. Put this bowl on top of another bowl containing boiling water and stir gently until dissolved. Leave until lukewarm.

Put the egg yolk, cheese, sugar and 125ml of the cream into a blender and blend until smooth. In another container fold together the finely chopped peaches, jam and gelatine then add the cheese mixture, and a further 125ml of cream. Fold together.

Whisk the egg white until stiff then fold into the cheese mixture. Pour on top of the amaretti base.

Leave in the fridge for two to three hours, or until set.

Serve with the remaining whipped cream and sliced peach.

Pudding

ortica e panna
Nettle cream

SERVES 6

This is a very old English recipe, eaten when tea was always at 5pm. It looks particularly pretty if you allow it to set in an old-fashioned jelly mould. (You can buy nettle tea, loose or in bags, at health food stores, or make your own by infusing the young shoots of nettle plants).

15g nettle tea, or 6 nettle tea bags
300ml milk
2 egg yolks
30g caster sugar
15g powdered gelatine
150ml double cream
Fresh fruit of choice to decorate

Put the tea leaves or bags and milk into a pan and bring to the boil. Remove from the heat, and allow to infuse for fifteen minutes, then strain, or remove the tea bags if using. Beat together the egg yolk and sugar, then mix into the milk. Dissolve the gelatine in a tablespoon of water for five minutes. Whip the double cream until standing in stiff peaks, then fold the milk, cream and gelatine together. Pour into a mould or bowl, and refrigerate for two to three hours, or until set. Turn out, and decorate with fresh fruit.

zabaglione

There is contention in Italy over whether zabaglione is a sweet, or a pick-me-up - it used to be given to people when they didn't feel well, and was actually served up to patients in hospitals! I first saw zabaglione when I was four years old, and my grandmother made it for my expectant mother.

The traditional, and best, alcohol to use is Marsala (*secco*, or dry) but I have also successfully used both Moscato wine, which is sweeter, and gives an aftertaste of Muscadet, and Barolo Chinato, a delicious concoction of Barolo fortified with quinine and herbs. Barolo Chinato is also a very good aperitivo, or after-dinner drink.

Zabaglione is a very luxurious pudding, which I like to serve in old-fashioned glasses with our Bicciolani biscuits (see page 71).

Per person:

3 egg yolks
100g sugar
25ml liquer

Briskly whisk the egg yolks and sugar in a bowl, stand over a pan of simmering water, making sure the bowl is not actually touching the water. Continue whisking until light and fluffy. Spoon into serving glasses or bowls.

Index

anguilla al barolo 49
asparagi 15
asparagi con gorgonzola 17
asparagi tradizionali 15
asparagus 15
asparagus with gorgonzola 17
asparagus, traditional Italian way 15
asparagus, with tagliatelle 17
astice con pesche gialle 49

baked pears in red wine with a sauce
of two classic Italian cheeses 19
baked turbot 43
barley risotto 33
beccaccia con crostone 61
bechamel sauce 12
beef fillet, marinated 17
bicciolani di vercelli 71
biscuits, vercelli 71
black pudding with onions 21
branzino del mulino 63
bunèt 73

calamari con la zucca 37
carpaccio di filetto 17
carpaccio di trota di mare affumicata 21
carpaccio of smoked sea trout 21
cheesecake, peach, with an amaretti crust 75
chicken la bella rosin 53
chicken, stuffed 53
chickpea and oxtail stew 57
chocolate, Piemontese dark, dessert 73
coniglio in padella 67
crema di torrone 71
cuttlefish risotto 35

eel in red wine 49
egg pasta 12
eggs with white truffles 19

filetto alla piemontese 55
fillet steak Piemontese-style 55
fish, mixed fried 47
fish stew, Scarborough 45
fritto misto di mare 47
fruit salad, Piemontese 73

gnocchi alla bava 31
gnocchi, potato, with 'dribble' 31

insalata di carne cruda alla monferrina 23

lingua di bue 59
lobster with peaches 49
luccio ai funghi 51

macedonia di frutta con le noci e maraschino 73
marinated beef fillet 17
meat, raw, salad Monferrato-style 23
mixed fried fish 47
monkfish stew with truffles 39

nettle cream 77
nougat cream 71

ortica e panna 77
orzotto 33
ox tongue with parsley sauce 59
oxtail, and chickpea, stew 57

pacchetti di fagiano fritti 69
partridge with black truffles 65
pasta con lumachine di mare 25
pasta, egg 12
pasta, egg, with winkles 25
peach cheesecake with an amaretti crust 75
pera cotta al vino rosso con salsa al gorgonzola e mascarpone 19
pernice al tartufo nero 65
pheasant, shallow-fried parcels of 69
pickled trout 23
Piemontese dark chocolate dessert 73
Piemontese fruit salad 73
pike with mushrooms 51
polenta concia 67
pollo alla bella rosin 53
pollo farcito 53
potato gnocchi with 'dribble' 31

rabbit in the pan 67
ravioli di cervo e tartufi neri 27
raw meat salad monferatto-style 23
risotto, barley 33
risotto con seppia e tartufi neri 35
risotto, cuttlefish and truffles 35
risotto in bianco con tartufo 41
risotto with white truffle 41
rombo al forno 43

salad, raw meat, Monferrato-style 23
salsa alla besciamella 12
sanguinaccio con cipolle 21
sauce, bechamel 12
sauce, white 12
Scarborough fish stew 45
sea bass of the mill 63
sea trout, smoked, carpaccio of 21
sea trout with horseradish 29
shallow-fried parcels of pheasant 69
squid stuffed with pumpkin 37

stracotto di coda di manzo e ceci 57
steak, fillet, Piemontese-style 55
stock, beef 11
stock, chicken 11
stock, fish 11
stock, simple vegetable 11
stufato di pesce di scarborough 45
stuffed chicken 53

tagliatelle agli asparagi 17
tagliatelle with asparagus 17
tajarin di meliga 33
tongue, ox, with parsley sauce 59
torta di formaggio alle pesche con crosta di amaretti 75
tripe 55
trippa 55
trota di mare con rafano 29
trota in carpione 23
trout, pickled 23
truffles, and cuttlefish risotto 35
truffles, and monkfish stew 39
truffles, black, with partridge 65
truffles, black, with venison ravioli 27
truffles, white, with eggs 19
truffles, white, with risotto 41
turbot, baked 43

uovo al tegamino con tartufi bianchi 19

venison ravioli with black truffles 27
Vercelli biscuits 71

white sauce 12
winkles, egg pasta with 25
woodcock with crusty polenta 61

yorkshire puddings 13
zabaglione 77
zuppa di coda di rospo al tartufo 39